D1463414

Meditation

Thorsons First Directions

Meditation

Christina Feldman

Thorsons
An Imprint of HarperCollinsPublishers
77–85 Fulham Palace Road,
Hammersmith, London W6 8JB

The Thorsons website is: www.thorsons.com

Published by Thorsons 2001

10 9 8 7 6 5 4 3 2 1

Text copyright © Christina Feldman 2001
Copyright © HarperCollinsPublishers Ltd 2001

Christina Feldman asserts the moral right
to be identified as the author of this work

Text derived from *Principles of Meditation*, published by Thorsons 1998

Editor: Louise McNamara
Design: Wheelhouse Creative
Production: Melanie Vandevelde
Photography from PhotoDisc Europe

A catalogue record for this book
is available from the British Library

ISBN 0 00711017 0

Printed and bound in Hong Kong

All rights reserved. No part of this publication may be
reproduced, stored in a retrieval system, or transmitted,
in any form or by any means, electronic, mechanical,
photocopying, recording or otherwise, without the prior
permission of the publishers.

Contents

Meditation

is an ancient method of achieving calm and

tranquillity

What Is Meditation?

Throughout history people have retreated to mountain tops, deserts and caves in order to meditate. Every culture and tradition in our world, from Asia to the Amazon, has created a system or discipline that helps us find an inner sanctuary of calmness, depth and wisdom. Something that also brings about altered states of consciousness, gives us an enhanced sense of the sacred and allows us to develop our own potential. Meditation is a direct response to the universal desire for oneness, wisdom and freedom. It is a path we can follow throughout our lives, with all their different demands and challenges, that can bring us calmness, depth and wisdom.

   Meditation affects both mind and body. It has become the path of countless people who seek spiritual renewal, well-being, and an enriched quality of life.

Before you begin to practise meditation you will have experienced glimpses of genuine meditation – moments when your mind is calm and still.

For example:
- you may be walking through a park when your attention is captivated by the sound of a bird and you listen wholeheartedly
- you may feel deeply touched by the sorrow or pain of a friend, and suddenly feel deep intimacy and openheartedness
- you are suddenly able to let go of anxiety and preoccupation and experience moments of oneness and clarity.

These are all moments of meditative experience. In these moments of stillness and calm you have a brief glimpse of the richness and harmony possible for everyone. These moments invite us to discover for ourselves the heart of meditation.

Meditation is no longer just for cloistered, religious communities but is readily available to everyone, regardless of their background or religion. You do not need to be a spiritual expert, religiously educated or belong to a particular tradition in order to meditate. But you must be willing to learn, to see clearly, and to be wholehearted in your path. There are many schools of meditation and thousands of different meditation styles. They have unique differences and fundamental similarities, but the one element they all share is an emphasis on direct and personal experience. No one can take this journey for us – every tradition of meditation emphasizes the need to join in directly and to see for ourselves.

Being here now

Meditation is essentially a 'present' moment experience. Although you will have goals, directions and aspirations, your practice will be focused on the moment you are in and not on promises of the future. Whatever is happening in this moment will start you on your path to understanding, calm and peace.

There are many different systems of meditation. Although each tradition emphasizes different aspects, they all share certain core values:

- Attention – to establish ourselves in the present moment with focus and simplicity.
- Awareness – to develop a consciousness that is light, unburdened, sensitive and clear.
- Understanding – to understand the forces that move us in our actions, speech, relationships and beliefs in order to gain deeper wisdom.
- Compassion – to not be narcissistic or self-interested. Compassion is the foundation on which we build love, integrity and respect into our lives.

All meditative traditions believe that it is understanding that frees us.

What Can Meditation Do For Me?

Meditation is the starting point on your journey of transformation.

Meditation can transform and awaken us. It can bring about change –
by increasing our understanding, compassion and clarity. Through
meditation practice we become increasingly sensitive and aware. Our
minds become calmer and clearer, our ways of seeing ourselves – our
minds, bodies, characters – become more intuitive and direct and we
begin to understand ourselves with greater depth and compassion. We
learn the art of simplicity and how to disentangle ourselves from the
knots of confusion, habit and tension. We learn how to become calm
and at peace with ourselves. This personal transformation means we

begin to approach our lives with increasing skillfulness, wisdom and care. The choices we make in our lives, our way of relating to other people and the events of our lives, become guided by sensitivity, mindfulness and calm.

Meditation brings us new feelings of stillness, oneness and grace, and sometimes startling depths of concentration, peace and unity. Our ability to think clearly and intuitively deepens, our potential for creativity grows and the inner calmness we discover is reflected in an increased calmness and harmony in our lives. On a moment to moment level, we begin to see clearly the ways we affect our world and the ways we are affected by it.

Through practising meditation our lives will be transformed:
- confusion turns to clarity
- entanglement turns to freedom
- discontent turns to happiness
- agitation turns to serenity.

Happiness

Although we are all looking for lasting happiness and peace, our lives are full of loss, disappointment, tension, illness and confusion. Often we try to find happiness through avoiding challenging situations or trying to create a 'perfect' world for ourselves where nothing is disturbing or unpleasant. Or we try to satisfy all our desires – more things, more achievements, more experiences. Through meditation we awaken to the fact that no matter how much we try and control our world there will always be change. This allows us to start looking for happiness and peace in new ways. We learn that there is a difference between pleasure and happiness and that no matter how much we acquire we cannot escape the possibility of loss. Our lives will always be a blend of the delightful and the challenging, the pleasant and the unpleasant, flattering and disturbing encounters, health and sickness.

Through meditation we start to look inside ourselves for the source of happiness.

What Do I Need to Start?

A moral code

Every meditative tradition rests on a strong moral or ethical code. If we spend our lives bringing harm or pain to ourselves or others, our minds will find it very hard to achieve serenity or compassion, being stuck instead in regret, guilt and unease. Meditation is not just about inner change – it is not possible to separate the quality of our meditation from the quality of our lives. If our lives are full of tension, conflict or remorse this will be reflected in our meditation. If they are filled with peace, understanding and sensitivity, this too will be reflected.

When we are engaged in unethical action or speech we feel disharmony, fear and anger. For example, a cosmetics company was worried about the high turnover rate among the staff who were involved in testing products on animals. To counteract this they invited an instructor to teach meditation as a stress reduction technique. This led to many of the staff resigning. The meditation had helped them to connect to the fundamental unease they felt about the nature of their work.

Meditation teaches us to:
- make sure our speech and actions are always truthful
- be honest with ourselves and others
- respect life and not harm anyone or anything
- keep our mind and body unclouded by intoxicants.

The right attitude

Many people start meditating because they have been inspired by the stories of great saints and mystics who have had profound spiritual experiences. Although it is important to be inspired, don't feel disappointed when your initial experiences do not bring similar results. Every moment should be greeted as your teacher, including the moments of boredom, restlessness and resistance. Most styles of meditation are simple but this does not mean they are easy. The attitude we bring to our meditation will profoundly influence our experience of it.

- You must be willing to learn.
- You must have patience, openness and acceptance.
- You must have the humility to accept the moments you falter.
- You need the inspiration to begin again in every moment.

Patience

When you start meditating you will probably discover your mind is bursting with thoughts, your body is restless or uncomfortable and your emotions are overwhelming! The moment you focus your attention it is swept away by memories, or planning the future, or lost in the mind storms of the present. Don't think that your meditation can only truly begin once you are rid of all of these distractions; this will only lead to tension and confusion. When you are faced with forces trying to pull you away from your meditation, patience will bring you again and again back to the moment you are in. No matter how lost you become in your thoughts, you can always start to cultivate awareness again in the very next moment.

Patience is one of the fundamental principles of meditation practice. It helps us to find calmness and harmony rather than struggle and tension. It is important, however, not to approach the preoccupations and thoughts that plague you as enemies – it is in the midst of these that you will learn some of the deepest lessons of your life. It is when we are disturbed and challenged that we learn most deeply about acceptance, balance and compassion.

Acceptance

Acceptance will help your meditation to deepen. True acceptance means being able to see things as they actually are, free from judgement or prejudice. If we want to change we must become more aware and sensitive to our inner landscape. Through meditation we become increasingly intimate with all the different thoughts, feelings, impressions and aspirations that shape us as human beings. We are not always happy with these different sides of us because they don't fit with our image of who we think we should be.

   This is why acceptance is important. It makes us more compassionate and generous, both towards ourselves and other people. We stop trying to justify, excuse or villify the feelings that arise. Understanding the unpredictable nature of our thoughts allows us to step back just a little, to refrain from judgement, to see things as they actually are and to stay balanced.

Simplicity

Simplicity is a principle found in all spiritual traditions. It allows us to be calm and wholehearted in our lives and within ourselves. Simplicity does not mean we abandon our lives, work and relationships, instead it looks at how we approach these areas of our life. It means disentangling ourselves from complexity, excess and confusion. We may have excessive possessions, commitments or thoughts – and if our minds are burdened then we won't feel calm and balanced. Cultivating a path of simplicity begins with taking an honest look at our lives. Doing too much, making too many commitments and wanting too much makes us tense and obsessive. We develop simplicity by learning to be simply present, attending wholeheartedly to the moment we are in. Simplicity teaches us to let go – in any moment of our lives it is not possible to attend to every detail of our past or future. We can only fully attend to the moment we are in, simply being in the moment.

Dedication

Dedication and perseverance are also essential. Meditation will bring moments of dazzling insight and bliss, but there will also be times when it seems that nothing is happening and our meditation is boring. Or we experience inner turmoil and painful states of mind. This is natural. There will be highs and lows, times of delight and times of challenge. Dedication and perseverance will sustain us on our journey and keep us balanced. Rather than despairing over a lack of progress or being assailed by inner thoughts we should instead remember our initial intentions and try to be present with whatever difficulty is before us. Meditation is concerned with awakening, and awakening embraces every part of our experience, whether pleasing or challenging.

Remember:
- don't judge
- don't reject
- don't conclude
- bring a calm, balanced attentiveness to everything that presents itself

How Do I Do it?

For meditation to be meaningful and effective it must be integrated into the daily rhythms of our lives. Most of us do not start meditating because we want to separate ourselves from the world – we do it because we want to know how to be present in ourselves and with our families. We want to approach work and play with greater wisdom and compassion. To bring meditation into our daily lives we should set aside special times for formal practice as well as applying this practice on a moment to moment level.

Time

We all have different lifestyles and commitments and no one can say there is a right amount of time to dedicate to meditation practice. Some people can only allow for a regular, daily practice, some can take an extended retreat. What is most important is to create a time in our day that is regularly dedicated to our meditation. Making these periods of meditation into a reliable part of our daily routine is invaluable. We may begin with fifteen-minute or half-hour periods – it is all worthwhile. Always approach these times with great care – they are not times for rehearsing our day or thinking about what we haven't done. These are times for focus and dedication.

When we wake in the morning or before going to bed at night are good times for stillness and reflection.

Where do I meditate?

It is a good idea to create a particular meditation space. This should have a certain simplicity that reminds us how important it is to take care of our inner selves. It may be simply a corner of our bedroom. If possible, find a place away from excess noise and disturbance, turn off the telephone and television and create a dedicated space of silence and calmness.

How do I sit?

Most of us have seen images of what meditation looks like in the form of Buddha statues, but this is not essential! Whether you choose to sit in a full lotus position or in a chair there are a few simple guidelines:

- Make sure you feel at ease and relaxed. Your meditation will not be fruitful if your body is very uncomfortable or tense. Experiment until you find a posture that you are able to hold without forcing.
- Sit with an upright back, whether this is on a cushion, on the floor or on a chair.
- Let your body relax, with your eyes closed or simply focused on the floor in front of you. Your body should feel alert and attentive.

Do I need a teacher?

Some traditions emphasize the need for a teacher more than others. A teacher will offer more than just instruction in technique or form, they can also be a spiritual friend, able to offer guidance and experience. As your meditation deepens, the support of someone who has travelled this path before you can be invaluable. However, a relationship with a teacher is not essential. If you bring the willingness to learn and the commitment to developing attentiveness, you have everything you need to begin.

Beginning to meditate

- Choose a regular time – morning, evening or whenever you can rely on not being interrupted
- Find a place – as secluded, simple and quiet as possible
- Choose a posture that is comfortable
- Set a minimum time for your meditation, whether it is 15, 30 or 45 minutes
- Check your body for any apparent areas of tension and consciously relax
- Take a few deep breaths
- Begin

Meditating With Concentration

All schools of meditation agree that we need to cultivate concentration. Retraining our attention is absolutely crucial – if we want to possess depth, balance and understanding we must first possess a clear and calm attentiveness. Concentration helps to simplify our minds. Rather than being captive to an endless stream of random thoughts, memories, plans and images, our attention deepens and our thoughts slow down and become clearer to us.

Concentration practice is not about trying to suppress your thoughts; it is only in very profound states of concentration that your mind will come to total stillness. Meditation is not anti-thought – in fact, concentration enables us to think more creatively and appropriately, rather than be dominated by excess thinking.

The benefits of concentration practice
- Learning to attend wholeheartedly to one moment at a time will boost your confidence.
- You will develop inner resources of energy, attentiveness, dedication and calmness.
- As you become calmer you will become less addicted to busyness and entanglement.
- Anxiety and stress levels decrease and are replaced by well-being and serenity.
- Greater awareness allows you to respond intuitively to life rather than being a slave of habit.
- You will become less agitated and more calm.
- You will become less confused and more clear.

Choosing an object

We practise concentration by focusing our minds on a single subject, which will differ according to the meditation style. It can be a visual object, a sound or the breath. The intention is to cultivate an undivided attentiveness. Your chosen subject will act as a steady anchor, a lifeline you will continually and gently return to each time you become lost amidst the swirls of your thoughts.

Almost anything will serve as a focus, but it is helpful to choose an object that is relatively simple and familiar to you. If you initially select an intricate mandala or complex series of phrases you are making things unnecessarily difficult. As your concentration skills develop you can choose increasingly complex subjects but in the beginning simplicity is the best way to find calmness.

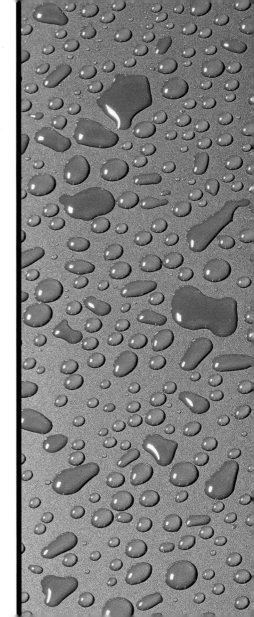

Be prepared …

Initially you will find that your attention repeatedly wanders away from your chosen subject, becoming lost in memories of the past, plans for the future or preoccupations in the present. You may no sooner return your attention to the present than it departs once more remembering a conversation you had yesterday. It is not unusual to feel that meditation has produced even more thoughts than before we began to practise – it is more likely you are simply becoming aware of the relentless nature of thought, produced by the mind untrained in attentiveness. The moment you notice that your attention has wandered away is the moment you return to attentiveness. Don't judge or become frustrated, simply anchor your attention once more in your meditation subject and begin again. Learning to be attentive requires the patience of a child learning to walk.

Good subjects for concentration meditation
A visual object – a flower, a candle flame, a symbolic object or shape
Sounds – a single word or phrase, chant or prayer
The breath – counting, naming or bare attention

Concentration with an image

First find a suitable place to practise, sit in a comfortable posture and adopt a spirit of patience and acceptance. Your visual subject may be a candle flame, a shape, a symbolic object, a mandala or a colour.

Settle yourself in a relaxed and alert posture, then place your chosen subject just in front of you. Gently settle your gaze and allow your mind and body to relax. Don't let your eyes wander around the room but simply fasten your attention upon the object. Whatever thoughts or bodily sensations arise, give them little attention – simply let them flow through you and pass away. As you begin to feel connected with your visual subject, let your eyes close and hold the visual impression of your subject in your mind. At first you may only be able to do this for a few moments. When the image becomes vague open your eyes and bring your gaze again upon the object. You may need to do this many times before you are able to hold the visual impression of your subject within your mind for longer periods.

As your concentration deepens you will find the image becomes more clearly imprinted upon your consciousness, increasingly clear in detail and vividness. The thoughts or images that previously clamoured for your attention will become quieter, like whispers arising and passing in the background of your consciousness. This is a sign that your concentration is deepening. Whenever you become distracted, know that you can always open your eyes and return to the direct visual connection with your subject.

Concentration with sound

Every spiritual tradition uses sound to cultivate concentration and devotion, whether it is through chanting the name of God or repeating classical phrases or prayers. A vast variety of sounds can be used to focus your attention. Mantras, prayers, phrases, chants and the repetition of symbolic religious words are all adopted. You can either verbally repeat the sounds, or say them silently to yourself. You can continually repeat the sound throughout your daily activities; or use it only during formal meditation.

   As with the previous exercise, the object is to turn your attention inward and focus wholeheartedly upon the sound. When you choose the sound remember to keep it simple and familiar.

Whether you choose the sound of OM or a simple prayer or inspirational quote, begin your practice with the slow and consistent repetition of it. Some people choose simple statements such as, 'May I be filled with compassion', or 'May all beings live in peace', but a single word such as 'peace' or 'calm' will serve the purpose. It is important that your repetition doesn't become mechanical or habitual and that each utterance is given wholehearted attentiveness. Again, when your attention becomes entangled elsewhere, cultivate your concentration by gently returning your attention to the sound. Your chosen sound or mantra can be used as a refuge of calm and focus whenever you feel stressed or confused.

Concentration with breathing

Breathing with mindfulness is one of the simplest ways of cultivating one-pointedness and concentration. It is free from religious connotations and therefore has a universal appeal, and there is nothing unfamiliar about it – breath is immediately accessible to us. No matter what else is happening in our lives, no matter what circumstances we find ourselves in, we are always breathing, so our breath is always available to us as an anchor of attentiveness.

As before, the aim is to cultivate a clear attentiveness and a calm mind, to establish us in the present moment and to bring serenity and joy. Like any other form of concentration practice, your breathing meditation can be developed into a deep state of absorption that can ultimately fill you with sublime joy. There are many different ways of concentrating through the breath – follow whichever feels best for you.

Concentration with counting

After settling your body in your chosen
meditation posture, turn your attention
inwardly so that you become aware of your
breathing process. Don't attempt to alter or
control your breathing – it will not help your
capacity to concentrate – but simply attend to
the natural rhythm of your breath. Counting
will help you focus your attention upon your
breath. As you breath in, silently count one, as
you breathe out count two. Continue up until
ten and then begin again with one. There will
be times when your attention becomes lost in
a thought process – the moment you become
aware of this simply return to counting one
and continue. Continue with the counting
until your attention begins to feel steady and
established in your breathing process and
then let it go, remembering that it is only a
tool to establish your attention.

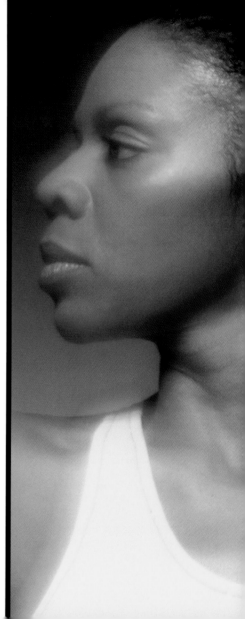

Concentration through fixing your attention

As you begin your meditation, first bring your attention to the whole movement of your breath from its beginning to end and notice the way in which your body responds to each inhalation and each exhalation. Notice in which part of your body you are most aware of your breath – it may be in the area of your upper lip and the entrance to your nostrils, the area of your chest or in the rise and fall of your abdomen. Establish your attention in the area where your breath is most noticeable and hold it there. Be aware of the sensations that arise in this area of your body as you breathe in and out, whether coolness, warmth, rising or falling – not evaluating them but bringing a mindful attentiveness.

Again, your attention will at times be pulled away by thoughts, sounds or sensations; the moment you are aware of this simply return your attention to the area of your body you have selected. As your mind calms and steadies you will notice changes both in the state of your body and in the rhythm of your breathing. Your body will begin to relax and feel lighter, your breathing will become more subtle and slow. Don't interfere in any way with this, but keep your attention unwavering upon your chosen focus.

Concentration with phrases

Some schools of meditation bond particular phrases to each breath. This bonding reminds us of the deeper objectives of our practice – we are aiming not just to become perfect breathers or just to achieve altered states of experience. We want to awaken our minds and to cultivate the qualities that will help us to live with greater wisdom and compassion. The phrases can vary enormously; some of those frequently used express particular qualities of heart and mind. As you breathe in you may silently repeat 'breathing in calmness', or 'breathing in peace', and silently repeat this on the out breath. You may choose a phrase like 'May I be filled with peace', or 'May I be free from fear'. Again, the same guidelines apply. Keep the phrases simple and use ones that genuinely express your aspirations for the meditation, the qualities you are searching for.

How to overcome obstacles

Concentration practice is simple but not easy. Inevitably you will meet obstacles – and these are the same forces of heart and mind that can create confusion in the rest of our lives. Meditation practice gives us the opportunity to learn to skilfully address these states, and we can integrate these skills into the whole of our lives. The obstacles that arise need to be accepted as part of our path and our practice. With attention they can be observed, penetrated and understood. With the right spirit they are not enemies to be overcome but doors to new ways of being and understanding. It is in these moments of challenge that our meditation becomes truly relevant – a pathway to peace and understanding.

- Being distracted makes our lives more fragmented and disconnected. We can lessen our tendency to distractedness through patience and perseverance.

- Dullness or sleepiness is a common problem. You try to focus your attention but feel sunk in heaviness, weariness or boredom. At times you are genuinely tired or stressed, at others this may be a form of resistance. When you start to feel dull, meditate for a time with your eyes open, check that your body is alert and upright, ensure your meditation space is not overly warm or stuffy or simply do your meditation practice standing up. When the mind feels sluggish it helps to use counting or naming to stay in touch with the breathing process.

- Restlessness can be the result of your mind being agitated and full, your body being restless, or your attention being unsettled and superficial. At these times make sure you bring to your posture an intentional relaxation and stillness. Notice where there is tension in your body and consciously relax. When restless, it is helpful to be more precise – counting or naming can help.

- At times we all question the worth of what we are doing, doubt our progress and feel we will never develop any depth in our meditation. This is natural and somewhat inevitable. Meditation is not a straight path of undiluted bliss and breakthrough. Doubt produces many thoughts which can undermine our confidence, effort and dedication. At such times it helps to remind ourselves of the aspirations we had when we began our practice and see this experience as a phase we are passing through.

- We want our experience to be different, to have different thoughts, experiences and feelings. We have ambitions, demands and expectations and our minds become filled with thoughts of what 'should' be happening. We want to reject the moment we are in and jump into a better, more ideal moment. This is when we need to remind ourselves that if we get through these moments of resistance we are developing some of the most important qualities of meditation – acceptance, harmony and understanding.

- Anger, judgement, resistance, prejudice and negativity will all reveal themselves to us as we practice. This does not mean we are spiritual failures, we are just becoming more aware of our inner landscape. If these feelings arise in our lives they will appear in our meditation. We should investigate them briefly – where do we sense anger in our bodies, how does it feel, what thoughts does it produce. We shouldn't try to avoid them, but include them kindly in the light of our attention.

Meditating With Mindfulness

Mindfulness is found within every great meditative tradition, from Buddhism to Sufism. Mindfulness helps us develop wisdom – by understanding more about ourselves and our lives. Mindfulness teaches us to shine the light of clear, mindful attentiveness upon every moment of our experience. One of its great benefits is that it can be developed and practised in any posture, in any circumstance.

For anything to change in our lives we must first be aware. Awareness is the key to transformation.

Mindfulness is quite different from concentration practice. Where concentration practice is exclusive, focusing upon a single object while excluding other aspects of our experience, mindfulness is inclusive. Whatever is happening in any moment can be subject to mindfulness. This form of meditation is like a wholehearted listening to whatever is going on inside and outside ourselves, without judgement or prejudice.

Bare attention

Mindfulness meditation teaches a form of concentration called bare attention. We bring bare attention to each moment of our changing experience – being fully present in that moment without distractedness or wavering. In mindfulness meditation you shift your attention with the moment-to-moment changes that occur in your experience. If you wish, the breath can still be your primary anchor, but you give equal attention to sights, sounds, thoughts, feelings and sensations as they emerge.

When your mind is settled calmly in the present moment it allows you to be deeply receptive and insightful. Slowing down the stream of inner busyness allows every moment to be highlighted in the light of greater sensitivity and clarity of vision. Insight will awaken and liberate you from the beliefs, prejudices and habits which blind you to seeing things as they truly are. Mindfulness brings you close to each moment.

Mindfulness meditation can be practiced in a variety of ways. But beneath the superficial differences, there are several essential principles found in all the different practices:

Sensitivity

Whatever presents itself to our attention in any moment is worthy of our wholehearted attention. Sounds, sights, thoughts or body sensations are all greeted equally. This means we must withdraw our judgements of good and bad – there is just what is, as it is. Bringing this clear attentiveness to every moment helps us see, listen, touch and feel more deeply and simply, and become much more sensitive.

Oneness

Sensitivity leads to a feeling of oneness with all the activities of our lives. When we walk we just walk without endlessly thinking about our destination. When we wash the dishes we do it with the spirit of mindfulness we apply to our formal meditation. When we listen to another person speak, we attend fully instead of being lost in all our conclusions about them. We become increasingly connected with the vitality and richness of each moment.

Clarity

The mindfulness we bring to each moment is not a vague, wandering quality of attention. It is clear and steady, attending to whatever is predominant in the moment – one sound at a time, one sensation at a time, one thought at a time. Mindfulness is like a mirror, simply reflecting without preference what is actually happening in each moment.

Present moment

Practicing mindfulness meditation keeps you in the present moment where thoughts of both past and future will arise and pass. Understanding allows you to be at peace with the past and enter into the next moment – the future – with confidence and ease.

Investigation

Mindfulness brings an investigative quality to our thought that helps our intuition develop. It allows us to see the essence of each moment and everything that occurs within it, free of any distorting factors. This investigation helps us understand not only what is happening to us in each moment – the sounds, sights, thoughts and events we encounter – but also what is happening within us in relationship to them. Mindfulness strips away the colouring of judgement, fantasy and fear with which we surround these events and lets us see them as they actually are.

Intention

We need the intention to be present, to understand all things as they actually are, free from any distortion. We want to be able to see clearly and awaken to a mindfulness that is very different from the kind of attention a burglar may bring to a break-in or a tightrope walker to crossing a bar.

Practicing mindfulness

There are many different styles of mindfulness meditation. The best thing about it is its flexibility – every moment and every situation is the right moment and situation to be clearly present and mindful. Here are a few of the most widely practised traditions. The principles of developing calmness, understanding and steadiness of mind run through them all.

Mindfulness of body

Adopt a posture that is relaxed, alert and still. Become aware of your entire body and the variety of sensations within it. Then bring your attention to the top of your head, concentrating on what is happening there. From there move your attention systematically down through the entire body to the tip of your toes. Don't try to make anything special happen; you are simply bringing mindful attention into the body, acknowledging the variety of sensations. Notice both the presence and absence of sensation, unpleasant and neutral sensations.

   In the beginning you will probably only experience a superficial perception – areas of pain or tension, heat or cold. As mindfulness deepens this will become more subtle, and you will become aware not only of the sensations within your body but also your relationship to them – how you react, whether you hold on to pleasant sensations, resist unpleasant and so on. Develop your practice by continually, steadily moving your attention through the body, from the head to the toes, without lingering upon or avoiding any area. As your practice develops your mind will no longer be dominated by the pull and push of sensation, preferences and reactions, and your entire life will include more understanding, happiness and balance.

Mindfulness with bare attention

First bring your attention to your breathing, either at the entrance to the nostrils or in the rising and falling of the abdomen. Focus on your breath within each moment but don't try to exclude anything else. Use your mindfulness to notice how your attention is drawn away from the breath to a sound, body sensation, feeling or thought. Bring bare attention to these moments, not considering them as distractions, but simply seeing them as they are – a thought as a thought, a sound as a sound, a sensation as a sensation. Make no judgements or attempts to analyse where they come from or why they are there. Simply be clearly present,

using bare attention, with whatever is uppermost in each moment. Then return to the focus of the breath. Bare attention gives us the ability to perceive each moment, just as it is, in an increasingly subtle way.

Mindfulness with noting

This is a similar practise that has the added ingredient of simply naming each moment. In harmony with the natural movement of the breath use a name to describe what is happening. If the breath is focused in the abdomen, mentally note 'rising' with the in-breath and 'falling' with the out-breath. If it is focused in the nose, note 'in-breath' or 'out-breath' with each inhalation and each exhalation.

This noting is useful for all moments when our attention is drawn away from the breath. Simply note to yourself 'thinking', 'hearing', 'feeling' to develop your attention clearly in each moment. As your mindfulness deepens you can become more precise – noting 'fantasy', 'memory', 'planning', etc, to clearly perceive what is happening in the moment. Note sounds simply with 'hearing' or 'listening', 'harsh' or 'soft'; sensation as 'pain' or 'pleasure'. This brings us closer to the moment, to understanding what is taking place within us.

Mindfulness in daily life

During our formal times of meditation we learn the skills of attentiveness, mindfulness, simplicity and understanding. These qualities can be brought into every part of our lives, giving us clarity, calm and wisdom. Meditation will have limited value if it is only practised in a particular posture or at a specific time.

To transform our lives, meditation needs to be applied in every moment and every circumstance. Special times or places put aside to be mindful will support and strengthen our ability to be present, clear and attentive in every moment.

Whenever we are moving, whether driving our car, eating or walking, we have a choice. We can spend these moments planning our next activity, reminiscing about the past or daydreaming, or we can bring a mindful attentiveness to them. Being wholeheartedly where we are, fully with what we are doing is the essence of mindfulness. The familiarity of our regular daily activities means we often dismiss them as not deserving of mindfulness, yet it is here that we become most prone to habit, dullness or reaction. These are the times when we can learn to be awake, sensitive and connected to whatever is taking place. Bringing wholehearted mindfulness to each moment fills it with vitality and life.

Meditating With Devotion

Every great spiritual tradition includes the principle of devotion; it is the most frequently practised style of meditation in our contemporary world. Tibetan Buddhists reciting mantras on their malas (prayer beads), Sufis dancing, Hasidic Jews meeting in prayer in a synagogue and Christians joining their voices in hymn or gathering together in silent prayer are all practising devotion. All the different rituals, festivals of thanksgiving and forms of adoration are ways of expressing devotion and of celebrating the divine.

Devotional meditation can be silent or vocal, with chants or prayers. It may be still or moving, with dancing or bowing; it may be practised in solitude or with others. The essence of all devotional practices is love. In theistic traditions the devotion is directed towards a spiritual deity or entity. In non-theistic traditions, such as Buddhism, it is cultivated through ritual and reflection. In every tradition devotion provides a way for people to gather and find support in collective meditation and celebration. Whatever form of devotion you practice, you will ultimately discover the qualities you thought were contained in the deity are actually within yourself.

The primary qualities you develop in devotional practices of meditation are:
- faith
- energy
- concentration
- surrender.

Practising devotional meditation

Concentration

Concentration is as key in devotional practices as in any other style of meditation. Here it is practised by meditating with your chosen subject of devotion, whether it is a mantra, visual symbol, prayer or divine entity. You focus your mind upon it, both in formal meditation and in all the activities of your day – your attention is repeatedly turned towards the mantra, prayer or visual symbol. Through the love and faith you bring to your devotion your mind gradually becomes increasingly engaged with the object of devotion, and other thoughts and habits will lose their power.

The principles of concentration previously discussed apply here. You will need patience and be willing to begin again in each moment. As your meditation deepens, the object of concentration, such as the mantra or symbol, will fade and your attention will be absorbed into the object of devotion. You will lose the sense of separation and eventually your whole consciousness and body will be taken up with joy and a sense of oneness with the object of your devotion.

You will also need faith, purity and an attitude of selflessness. Faith inspires us on every journey we make in our lives, whether we are trying to climb a mountain or undertaking a spiritual path. Purity of conduct, heart and mind are particularly important in devotional practice. The focus of our devotion symbolizes the purity we are aspiring to, and by keeping our attention focused on the qualities of the divine we start to become less self-centered. Devotion and practice allow the qualities of purity that initially we see in the focus of our devotion to be awakened within our own hearts and minds.

The styles of devotion vary in different traditions, but they all hold one-pointedness, reflection, purity and selflessness at their heart.

Mantras

Mantras are popular styles of devotional practice, found in many spiritual traditions including Christianity, Buddhism and Hinduism. Different traditions use different mantras, such as 'Hare Krishna', 'Namo Buddhia', 'Kyrie Eleison', 'God is love', 'Lord Jesus Christ, have mercy on me', or 'Om mane padme hum'. The mantra is often a single phrase from the scriptures that represents their desire to be awakened and liberated – and it must be meaningful, or the repetition will become a habit. The mantra is sometimes chanted aloud, sometimes repeated silently. By consciously, mindfully repeating the mantra we celebrate and remember the divine. This remembrance and reflection makes the mantra into a devotional practice rather than purely a concentration practice.

Prayer

Prayer is the most frequently practised style of meditation in the Christian tradition. Prayer encourages us to open our hearts and minds and embrace a higher understanding. Equally, it calls for the same qualities of humility, sincerity, self-discipline and ethics that form the central core of all meditation styles. As with mantras, our practice of prayer can be silent or verbal, in solitude or as part of a community, in formal meditation or something that permeates all the activities of our day. The constant remembrance of God fills our hearts and minds with love, faith and perseverance. The concentration developed through prayer brings the mind to stillness and joy.

Visualization

Visualization is both a powerful concentration practice and a way of practicing devotion. When used purely as a concentration practice the object of visualization is often neutral, such as a candle flame or a simple picture. When it is also used for devotion the object will generally be a symbol, picture or deity – something that has spiritual

significance. Visualization subjects are often chosen that represent certain qualities of heart and mind we wish to cultivate within ourselves, such as wisdom, purity or compassion. Visualization should be practiced alone during your moments of formal meditation. First, place a picture of the symbol or deity in front of you so you can make a visual connection with the picture and it becomes familiar. Then close your eyes and try to recall the symbol in your consciousness. At first the picture is often difficult to recall, or it appears in a very vague way. If so, open your eyes and make the visual connection again. Eventually you will be able to recall the symbol in your consciousness easily and clearly and to hold it for longer periods of time.

Ritual

From earliest times every culture has created many different rituals, in a variety of different forms, as a way to cultivate faith and devotion. Joining in a ritual gives us the opportunity to be part of a community and to find support through being with others on similar paths. Ritual also gives us something visible to aspire to. We live in a world where we are constantly bombarded by symbols encouraging us to possess more, acquire more, be more successful, improve our appearance. This is why the symbols of wisdom, compassion and awakening we find in spiritual ritual are becoming increasingly important.

Forms of ritual include:
- chants
- blessings
- offerings
- prayers
- events that mark important life changes such as birth and death.

Rituals aim to give us a deep sense of connection with a tradition and teaching. They are only meaningful when we approach them with sincerity, sensitivity and mindfulness. Then they will remind us that our own meditative path is part of a greater community and tradition. When a community comes together to bless and welcome a new child with flowers and prayers, to celebrate the coming of age of an adolescent, or to plant a tree in memory of someone who has died, everyone is strengthened. Rituals do not need to be complicated – you may like to take part in simple rituals such as lighting a candle at the beginning of your meditation, or take a few moments at the end to dedicate your meditation to universal well-being, or to ring a bell, or to bow. All ritual is as meaningful as the depth of heartfulness and sincerity we bring to it.

Meditating to Calm Your Mind and Body

Meditation is not just a mystical path – it is profoundly practical. Through meditation we can learn how to feel calm and full of well-being in the midst of the stress, disappointments, illness and pain we all inevitably experience. We can learn to heal ourselves; our bodies, minds and emotions – not through avoiding or suppressing unpleasant feelings but through mindfulness and understanding.

Our world is full of stress and tension, anxiety, apprehension and confusion. Illness, pain and loss are part of the human condition and the lifestyles we lead often create more stress – deadlines, the

demands of work or lack of work, finances, competitiveness, ambition, fear of failure. Relationships can also be a source of stress, including our relationships to food, self-image, criticism and goals. Stress makes us anxious, uneasy, tense and reactive. If you often become impatient and angry with people; anxious about new challenges; wake in the morning with a sense of dread, or react to small disappointments with a sense of disaster, you are caught in a spiral of stress.

These feelings are a reminder that we need to give greater care and attention to the quality of our lives. Although we often have no control over events and encounters, we are not powerless in the ways we respond to them. Whether challenges make us stressful and devastated, or whether we can meet them with calmness and understanding, greatly depends on the quality of mindfulness and well-being we bring to them. If we try to disconnect from stress by overindulging in food, alcohol, drugs or entertainment all we do is camouflage our distress. We often engage all our senses in consuming – eating, listening to music, reading and moving all at the same time – and we call this activity relaxation!

Are you stressed? Are you subject to ...

• sleeplessness
• frequent headaches or neck pain
• overreactions to small challenges and intrusions
• repetitive or obsessive thinking
• feelings of anxiety or dread, of being overwhelmed
• overeating, or overindulgence in alcohol or drugs?

Meditation is not a magical cure-all for stress, but it does help us learn how to respond skillfully to the demands of our lives. Rather than avoiding stress or trying to find instant solutions it teaches us to look at the conflict or confusion with mindfulness, acceptance and understanding. Equally, meditation does not promise to eliminate pain or cure illness, but it can teach us how to find calmness and peace even in the midst of our pain.

Meditation has always recognized the connection between body and mind and this is now being acknowledged in medicine and science. Health is no longer seen as just a bodily state but something that includes both mind and body.

Pain and your emotions

Emotional pain causes as much suffering as illness and debilitation. Remember a time when you have been gripped by anger, furious at another person or event. Even after you have physically left the person or event you still carry residues of the encounter. You feel remorse, resentment and stress in both mind and body. When you physically tighten and tense you trigger a series of physiological events that lead directly to stress. Giving mindful attention to what is actually happening in your body helps you cut through the turmoil of your thoughts rather than being swept away by them. You will begin to feel calm, accepting, clear and focused. Now remember a time of great happiness in your life – a time when you felt deeply connected with nature or another person. Your mind will be soft and open, your thoughts calm and loving, with a heightened quality of awareness. Your body will relax and calm.

The habits and reactions that cause us to store stress in our bodies can be undone through attention and mindfulness. By learning to know our bodies and minds intimately we can achieve calmness, peace and harmony. Meditation helps us to stop feeling out of control or powerless by teaching us calmness and attention. Rather than being lost in fear, mindfulness allows us to become deeply interested in situations, events and encounters.

As our lives become more and more demanding we need to spend more and more time cultivating calmness and mindfulness. These times are not luxuries but a necessity if we value health, peace and understanding. And being calm or mindful never means we will lose the skills we need to meet the demands and busyness of our lives. The truth is that we are most creative, organized and productive when we are calmly established in mindfulness.

Being where we are

Reducing stress and achieving a state of calm doesn't come just through taking time out to meditate. We also need to be more aware and sensitive when we are in danger of becoming lost in mental activities, busyness or preoccupation – this is when we build up stress. Awareness always encourages us to 'be where we are' rather than trying to arrive somewhere else. As described earlier, it means giving calm and sensitive attention to every moment, every task and every interaction. This principle can be applied to every moment of our day to enable us to live calmly rather than stressfully.

Times for stillness

Beginning and ending our day with a time dedicated to stillness and attention is of enormous value in our lives. It helps us to approach each day with calmness and end each day with a sense of completion and mindfulness. Even giving fifteen minutes to meditation when we get up in the morning and before we go to sleep has a profound impact upon the quality of our mind and body.

Chronic pain

Increasingly meditation is being recognized as an effective way to alleviate chronic pain conditions. Chronic pain differs immensely from acute pain, which happens when we stub our toe, have a dose of flu or break an elbow. Acute pain is time-limited – it can be cured and it will end. However, chronic pain does not always have a recognizable cause and the point at which it will end is unknown. Chronic pain has become part of life for increasing numbers of people. It causes tremendous stress and this is where meditation is particularly effective. The calmness and understanding we can find using meditation to ease our pain can drastically reduce the levels of suffering that become associated with it.

By practicing meditation with breathing and body-mindfulness (see earlier chapters) we can break down the painful areas of the body and explore them in detail with a calm attentiveness. Pain is a tapestry of sensations that ebb and flow, with points of intensity which change from moment-to-moment. Using meditation to alleviate pain requires immense patience and commitment. There will be days when it is deeply effective, other days when it appears to make little difference. Consistently and patiently bringing a meditative approach to chronic pain will transform our relationship to it – it becomes our teacher, allowing us to learn deep lessons about acceptance, openness and balance.

Meditation to help a painful back

Our backs are most frequently the subject of chronic pain and tension. Lie down on your back in a comfortable posture. After taking a few deep breaths, bring your attention directly to the area of your back where there is pain. First, with your attention, trace its outlines. Learn the areas where it begins to fade or end. Bring your attention gently into the area that is painful. Notice if there are points of particular intensity and gently explore them with your attention. Notice the way the sensations change, intensifying and fading. Stay present as long as you can with a gentle, interested attention. If the sensations feel overwhelming move your attention into a calmer place in your body for a time, such as your hands or your breathing. As you relax, bring your attention again to your back. Approach these sensitive areas without feeling that the pain should change or disappear. Cultivate a calm and sensitive interest.

Breathing

Our breath is a great ally when we want to cultivate calmness and balance through our day. In any moment we can reconnect to it to restore steadiness and attention. No matter where we are or what we are doing we can always take a moment to pause and breathe with mindfulness. Learning to check in with our breath at regular intervals during the day is a direct way of checking in with the quality and state of our mind and body. It returns us to the present moment and gives us the opportunity to let go of tension and stress.

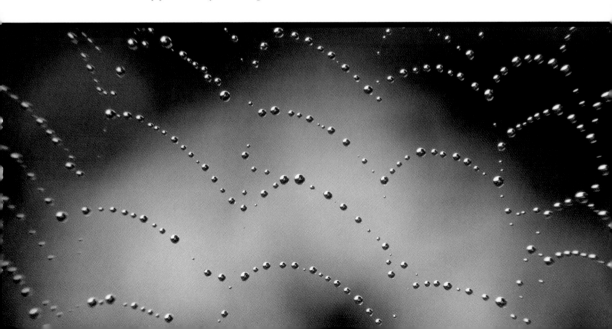

Calming breathing exercise

This exercise is great for easing tension and constriction. First find a posture that your body finds completely calming and relaxing. It is often helpful to lie down and place your hand on your abdomen or chest to reinforce your connection with your breathing. Initially, just notice how your breath moves in your body without forcing it in any way. Whether your breath is shallow or deep, simply pay attention to its movement and the way your body responds to it. Then consciously take a few deep breaths. Again, relax and let your breathing find its own natural rhythm. As your mind and body relax your breath will become both slower and deeper. If you find that your attention again becomes entangled in thoughts, images, memories or plans, take a few fuller breaths to establish your attention once more in your body. This is a direct and simple way of letting go of knots of tension that have accumulated in your body and mind.

Cultivating well-being

'Not enough time' has become the mantra of our culture. To achieve well-being, sensitivity and calmness we may need to carefully examine our whole approach to our lives. Do you have unrealistic expectations about how much you should achieve in a single day? This will create a stressed body and an overburdened mind. We must be clearly realistic about what it is possible for us to address in any moment. Preparing to go into your day with mindfulness and sensitivity in the simple tasks of dressing, showering and eating helps slow down a busy mind. Take moments throughout the day to check on what is happening in your body, giving attention to your shoulders, face and posture. Become aware of where you are storing tension and where you can relax. Use your breaks as times of simplicity and calmness – walking, breathing, listening. Stop rushing from one task to the next. There are many ways we can find calm in each day and if we value health and well-being we need to discover them.

Doorways to calm

- Choose an activity that is a regular part of your day, such as climbing the stairs or talking on the telephone, and intentionally approach it with calm and mindfulness.
- Learn to pause and breathe mindfully at the end of each task before going on to the next.
- Remember to check in with your body at regular intervals during the day. Pay particular attention to your shoulders, face and hands. Learn to relax.
- Take the time to eat slowly and mindfully.
- Become aware of the moments when your attention becomes fragmented – listening to music while reading, talking to someone while planning your next task. Explore what wholehearted attention means.
- Find moments in which you can be still.

Meditation in Daily Life

Meditation would have limited value if it were restricted to experiences achieved in formal sessions on a cushion. Meditation should transform all of your life, bringing calmness, well-being and balance to every moment and circumstance. It does not promise an 'ideal' world where we are never disturbed or challenged, but empowers us to live in the 'real' world with awareness and understanding.

Awareness is more than an exercise, it is a journey of a lifetime.

Formal meditation practice

Our daily meditation practice requires both discipline and effort yet it is the cornerstone of integrating meditation into the rest of our lives. Longer periods of formal meditation in retreats or courses which will give you guidance and a sense of community are also immensely valuable. There are many different organizations that offer a range of retreats and courses dedicated to meditation (see Resource Guide). Even if you are not interested in these or do not have the time available, it may be possible at times to take an afternoon or a day that you reserve entirely for meditation practice. Spending periods of time alone, developing calmness and stillness, and exploring your meditation practice can have a significant impact upon the rest of your week.

Walking

Walking is an integral part of our day, a simple activity that can become an exercise in mindfulness. Give attention to all the subtle shifts that are involved in taking a single step, in the sensation of your foot touching the ground. Walking helps us to integrate our minds and bodies. This very ordinary activity can be transformed through attentiveness into a time of sensitivity and wakefulness. As we walk in our day, we can be walking our meditative path.

Mindful eating

Preparing food and eating can also be times of deep sensitivity and awareness. Try to adopt the discipline of mindful eating – ensuring that you always sit down to eat, that you approach this time calmly and slowly and with the intention to be fully present. Take a moment to savour and finish each mouthful of food before you lift your fork to take the next. Bring mindful attention to the taste and sensations of everything you eat. Be aware of your posture, ensuring that your body is relaxed and at ease. Experiment with reserving one meal in the day to eat in silence. As you bring attention to these times the ordinary events in your lives are transformed – your body, mind and the present moment are unified.

Breaking habits

A powerful way to bring awareness and sensitivity into the activities of your daily life is to focus attention upon areas where you find yourself most prone to habit. Simply select one area of your life that you give little attention to because it is so familiar – the way you dress, the time you travel to and from work, the way you walk or sit, the way you speak to people. Then approach this activity as if you have never done it before. Give careful attention to how you use your body, the movements of your hands, the way you listen or your speech. You are not trying to find the 'right' way to do the activity, but to discover the way in which the simple, ordinary activities of your life can be transformed by attentiveness.

Inspiration

Inspiration and interest are essential if you want to develop and sustain your spiritual journey. It is easy to feel both interested and inspired when your meditation experiences are rich and fruitful, when you are experiencing dramatic insights. It is far more challenging to remain interested and inspired when your meditation feels flat or dry.

Mindful reading is one way to get more nourishment. To read in a reflective way, choose a book that is meaningful to you and use it as a basis for contemplation. Perhaps stay with a single line or chapter that speaks to your heart for a prolonged period of time. As you read, question the ways in which the message relates to your own experience.

Formal meditation, meeting with like-minded people, spending time in nature and reflection are all ways of awakening and keeping us interested in our meditative journey. Just as plants need the nourishment of soil, water and sun to grow, so our own meditation practice is dependent upon the nourishment we provide.

Resource Guide

The centres listed here do not expect you to have any particular religious affiliation nor will they try to impose any:

Australia

Dhammananda Forest Centre, Bodhi Farm, The Channon, Via Lismore, NSW 2480.
Contact for programme of retreats offered.

Canada

Westcoast Dharma Society, 2224 Larch Street, Vancouver, BC V6K 3P7.
Primarily offers weekend non-residential retreats and affiliated with a larger meditation group that offers classes and longer retreats.

France

Tapovan Forest Retreat, Marses, 11300 Festes, France.
Contact for programme of retreats offered.

Communauté de Taize, 71250 Taize, Saone-et-Loire. Tel: +33(0) 85 50 18 18.
An ecumenical spiritual centre open all year to people from all backgrounds.

Plum Village – Village des Pruniers, Meyrace, 47120 Loubes-Bernac. Tel: +33(0)16 53 96 75 40.
A Zen-Vietnamese centre under the guidance of Thich Nhat Hanh. Various retreats and opportunities to participate in the life of the resident community are available through the year.

Germany

Buddha-Haus Stadtzentrum, Klarastrasse 4, 80636 Munchen. Tel: +49(0)89 1238868.
A Theravada centre that offers a range of opportunities to learn meditation in weekend, day-long and longer seminars.

Haus der Stille, Muhlenweg 20, D-21514 Roseburg über Buchen. Tel: +49(0) 04158 214.
Offers a wide range of residential retreats drawing on all traditions of Buddhism. Comprehensive meditation instruction offered.

Seminarhaus Engl, Engl 1, 84339 Unterdietfurt. Tel: +49(0)8728 616.
A retreat environment offering a varied programme that draws upon all traditions.

Zentrum für Buddhismus, Waldhaus am Lachersee, D-56643 Nickenish.
A comprehensive range of non-sectarian residential retreats offered through the year. Write for programme.

Italy
AMECO, Via Valle di Riva 1, 00141 Roma.
Organizes a wide range of classes and retreats in Rome and elsewhere in Italy. Write for information.

The Netherlands
European Buddhist Union's European Buddhist Directory, EBU c/o BUN, PO Box 17286, 1001 JG Amsterdam.
For comprehensive listing of centres and meditation teaching throughout Europe.

Vipassana Meditation Foundation (Theravada), Kamerlingh Onnesstraat 71, 9727 HG Groningen. Tel: +31(0)50 5276051.
Offers retreats and classes with meditation instruction based on the Theravada tradition of Buddhism.

New Zealand
Te Moata Meditation Centre, PO Box 100, Tairu. Tel: +64 7868 8798.

South Africa
Buddhist Retreat Centre, PO Box 131, Ixopo 4630. Tel: 0336 341863.
Offers a range of retreats and instructions in meditation in a year-round programme.

Switzerland
Dhamma Gruppe, Postfach 5909, CH 3001, Bern.
Co-ordinates an ongoing retreat programme in Switzerland and throughout Europe led by a variety of different teachers. Write for schedule.

United Kingdom
Amaravati Buddhist Monastery, Great Gaddesden, Hemel Hempstead, Hertfordshire HP1 3BZ. Tel: 01442 843239.
A Theravada Buddhist centre which offers instruction and guidance to both beginning and experienced meditators under the guidance of resident monks and nuns. Has several affiliated monasteries and centres in England and around the world.

The Buddhist Society, 58 Eccleston Square, London SW1V 1PH. Tel: 020 7834 5858.
Aims for impartial presentation of main Buddhist tradition in the form of classes and activities. Offers an extensive library and provides information about the variety of Buddhist centres in England.

Gaia House, West Ogwell, Newton Abbot, Devon TQ12 6EN. Tel: 01626 333613.
Gaia House is a registered charity offering a wide range of residential retreats varying in length from a weekend to a month that are open to people from all backgrounds and are suitable for beginning and

experienced meditators. *The meditation instruction draws from all the main Buddhist traditions without the imposition of any religious belief. Also offers day-long meditation retreats in London and has a wide network of meditation groups.*
Call or write for retreat programme.

The National Retreat Centre, 24 South Audley Street, London S1Y 5DL. Tel: 020 7493 3534.
This is an ecumenical resource centre which provides information on Christian retreat houses and programmes around the country.

Ramakrishna Order, Unity House, Blind Lane, Bourne End, Buckinghamshire SL8 5LG. Tel: 01626 26464.
A Hindu Inter-faith temple that welcomes people from all faiths for private and group retreats.

Throssel Hole Priory, Carrshield, Hexham, Northumberland NE47 8AL. Tel: 01434 345204.
A Soto Zen meditation centre offering a range of retreats and meditation instruction. There are a large number of affiliated groups around the world. Introductory courses for beginners.

United States
Insight Meditation Society, 1230 Pleasant Street, Barre, Mass 01005. Tel: 978 355 4378.
Offers a year-round programme of meditation retreats open to people from all backgrounds and suitable for beginning and experienced meditators.

Spirit Rock, 5000 Sir Francis Drake Boulevard, PO Box 909, Woodacre, CA 94973.
Tel: 415 488 0164. *Offers both a widely-varied community and a retreat programme primarily based in the Buddhist tradition but open to people of all backgrounds and ages.*

Dr Jon Kabat-Zinn, Stress Reduction Program, University of Massachusetts Medical Center, 55 Lake Avenue, North, Worcester, MA 01655.
The Stress Reduction and Relaxation Program is a leading innovator in the integration of meditation into health care and high tension environments such as prisons. For further reading and information contact the above address.

Zen Centre of San Francisco, 300 Page Street, San Francisco, CA 94102. Tel: 415 863 3136.
Offers a variety of instruction opportunities and retreats in the Soto Zen tradition. Also has a range of affiliated communities and centres.

The centres listed may not have a retreat that suits you but they can be a valuable resource for further contacts. There is a wide variety of publications available for further information. Among these are:

The Buddhist Directory by Peter Lorie and Julie Foakes. Published by Newleaf, an imprint of Macmillan Publishers.

The Good Retreat Guide by Stafford Whiteaker. Published by Rider, an imprint of Random Century Group.